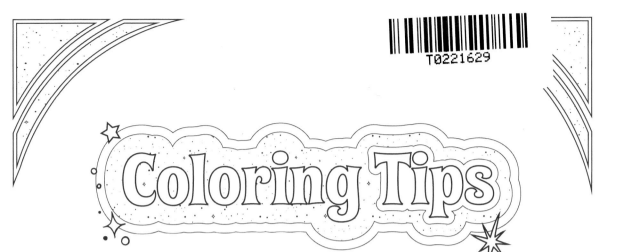

Coloring Tips

✧ This book is meant for all ages and skill levels! Use crayons, markers, gel pens, or whatever you have! Don't be afraid to mix your materials.

✧ There are no rules! Don't be afraid to color outside the lines or use every color of the rainbow.

✧ Use the test pages in the back of the book to test the colors of your markers or gel pens.

✧ When coloring with a marker, place a piece of thick paper under the page to prevent the color from bleeding through to the next page.

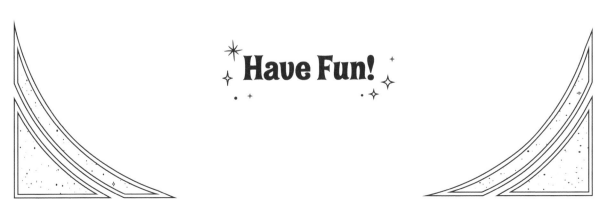

Have Fun!

Coloring
the
Zodiac

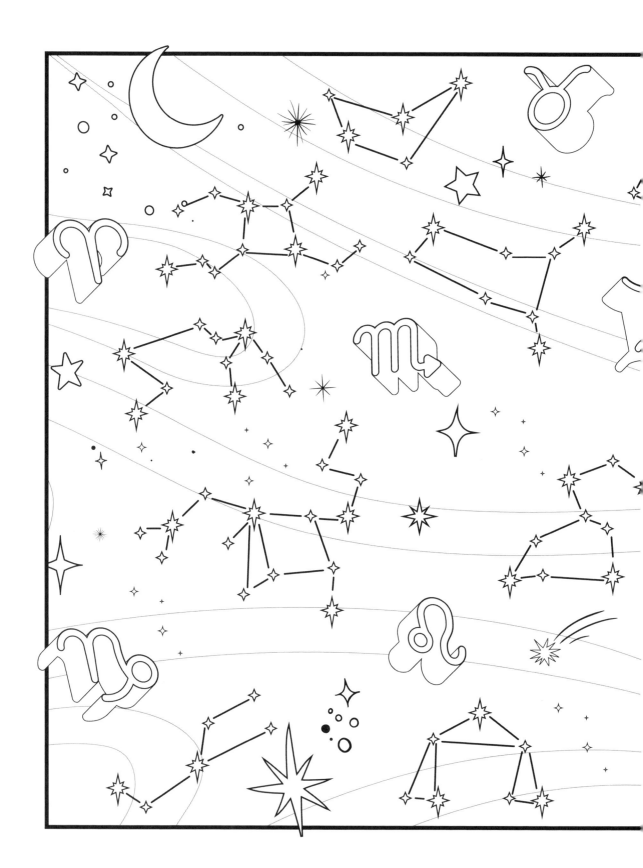

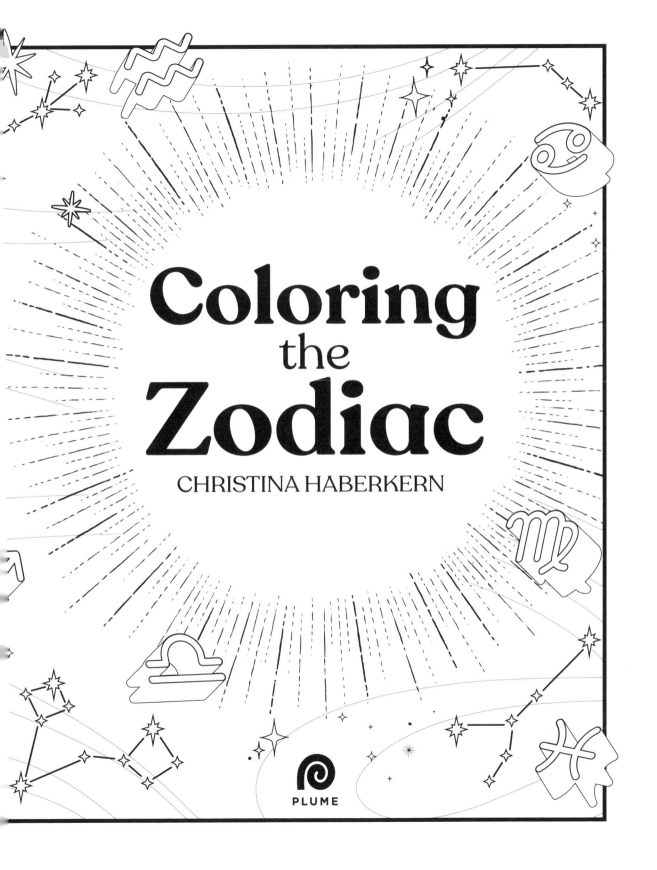

Coloring
the
Zodiac

CHRISTINA HABERKERN

PLUME

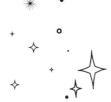

PLUME

An imprint of Penguin Random House LLC
penguinrandomhouse.com

PLUME and P colophon are registered trademarks of
Penguin Random House LLC.

LIBRARY OF CONGRESS CATALOGING-IN-PUBLICATION DATA
has been applied for.

ISBN 9780593186954 (paperback)

Printed in the United States of America
1st Printing

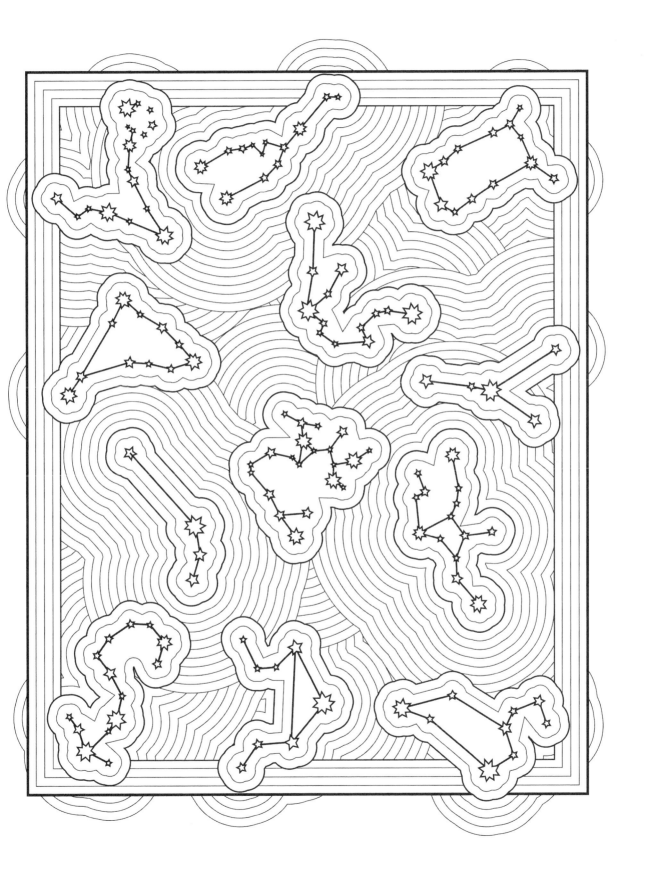

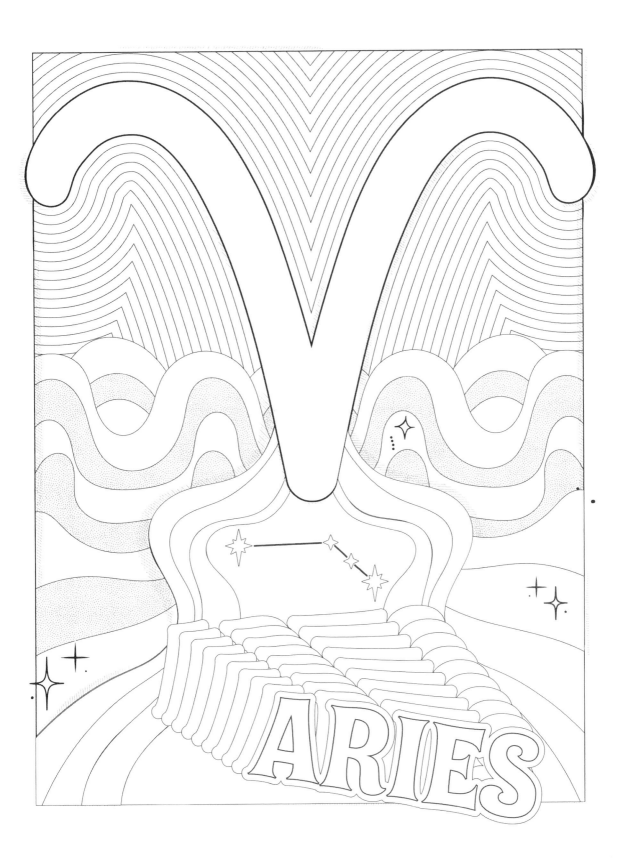

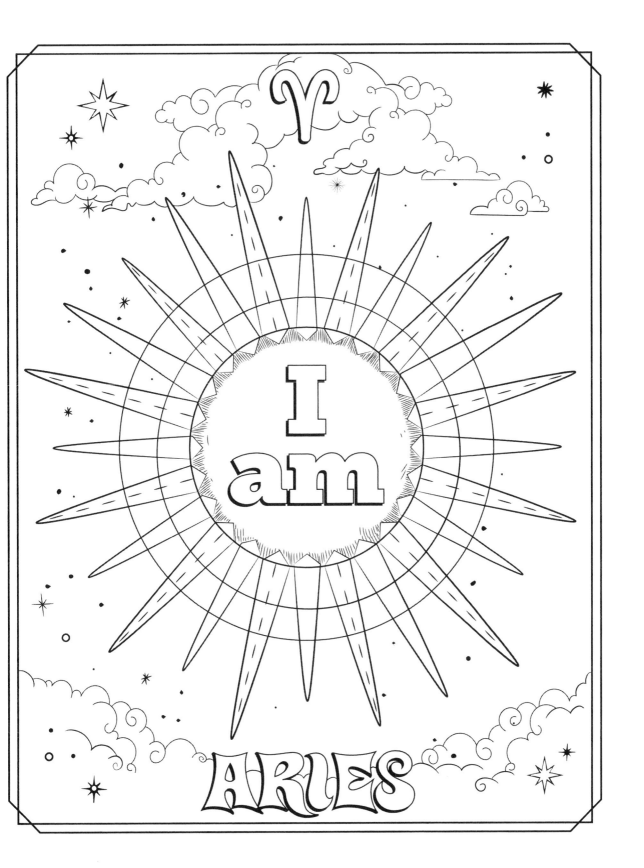

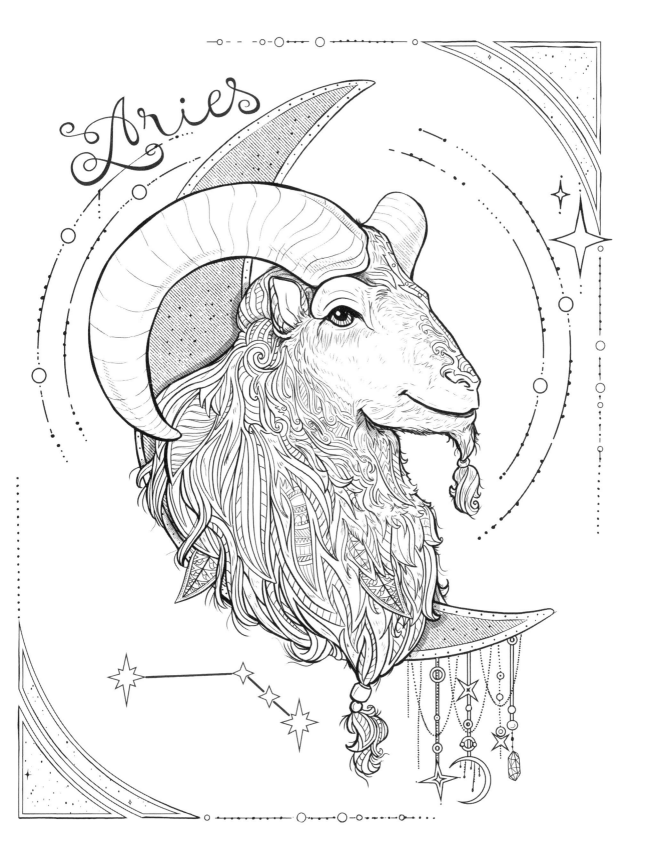

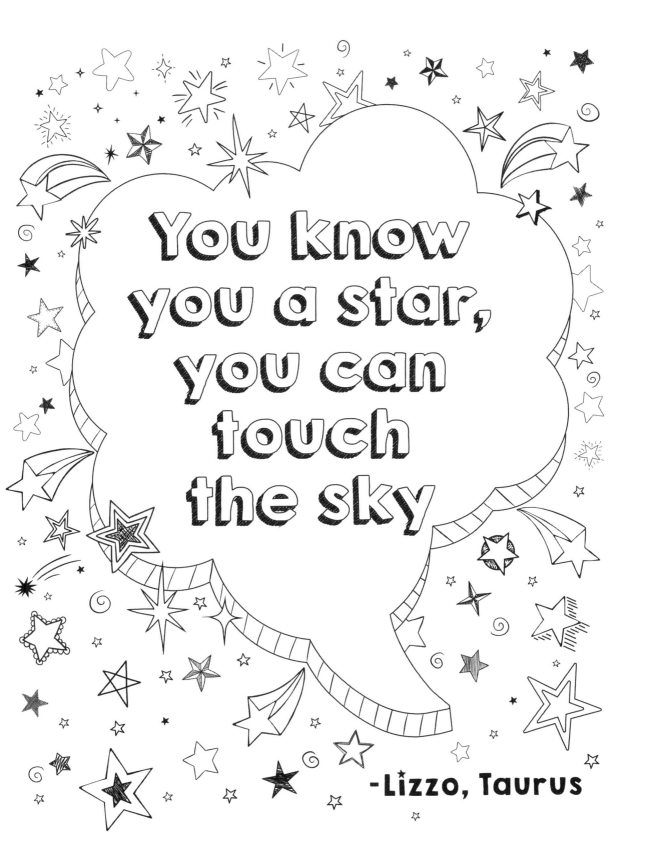

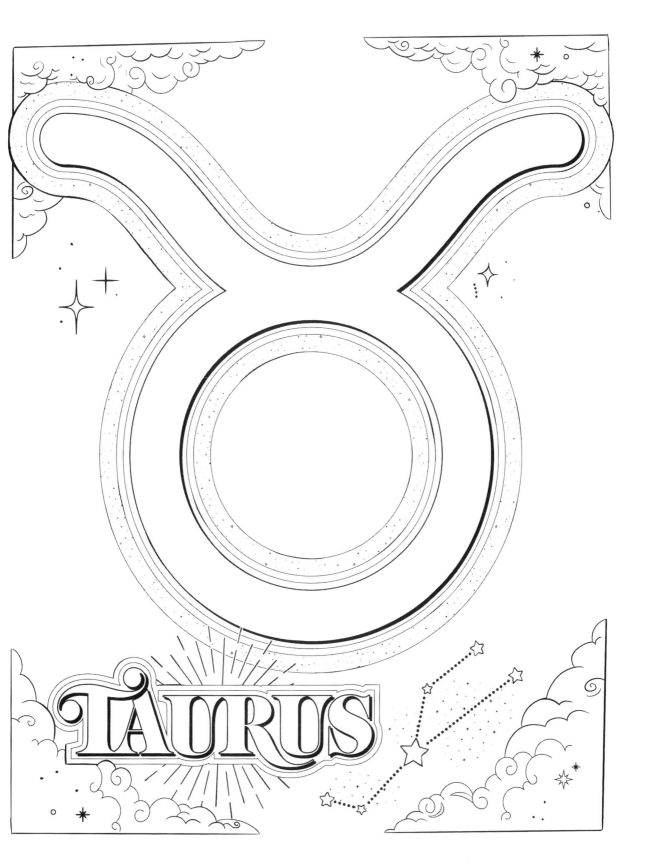

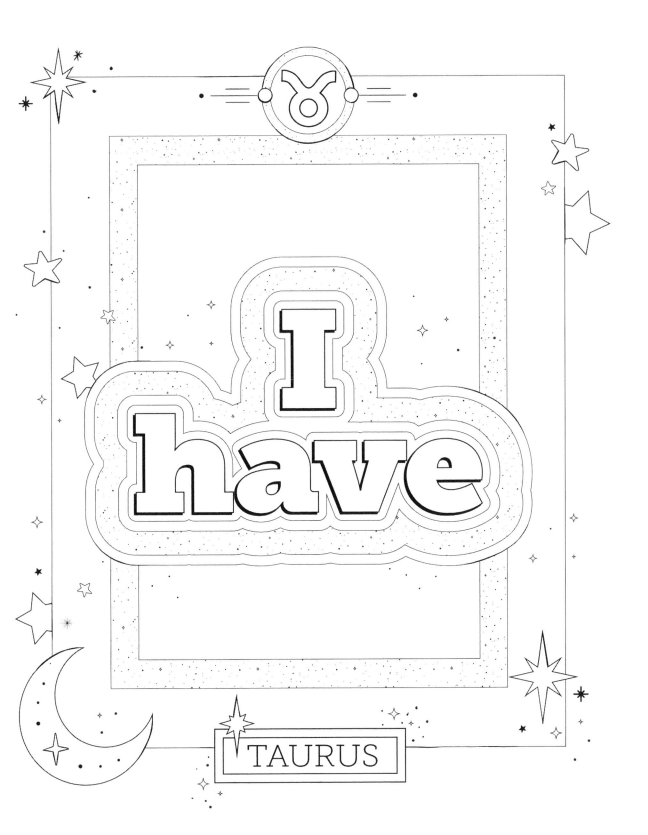

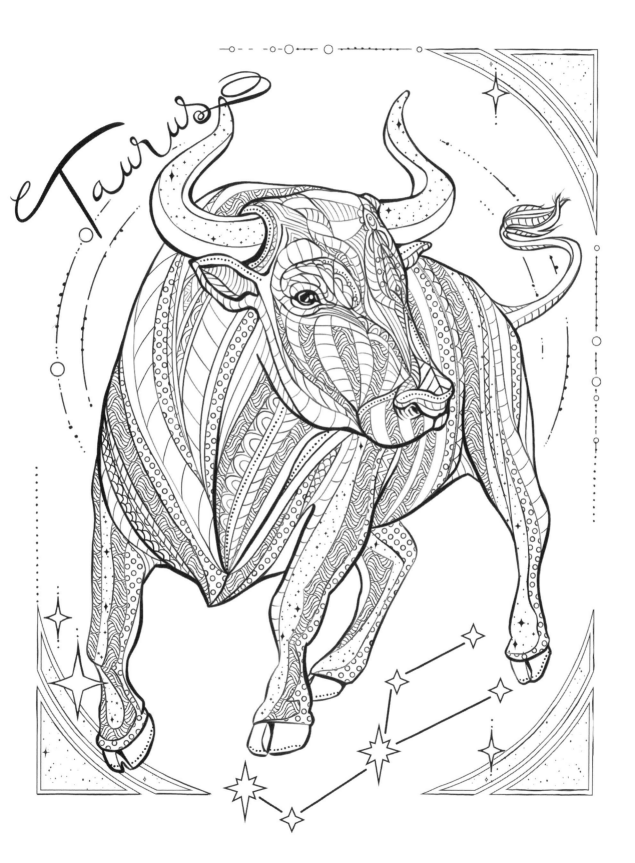

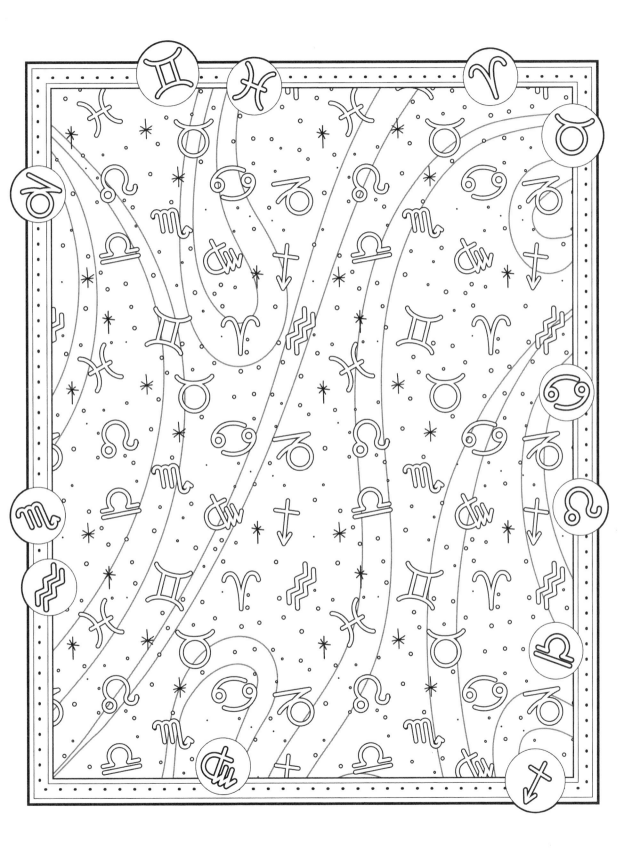

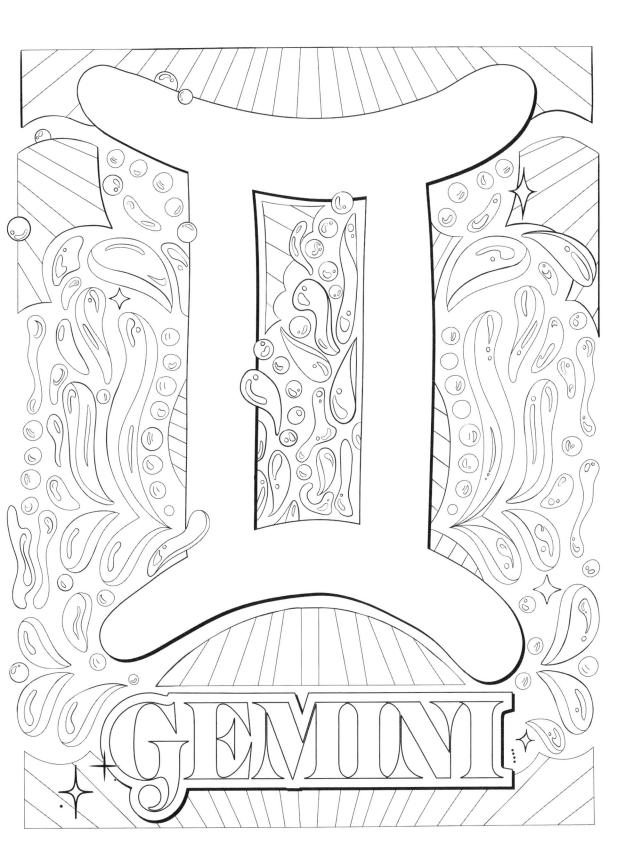

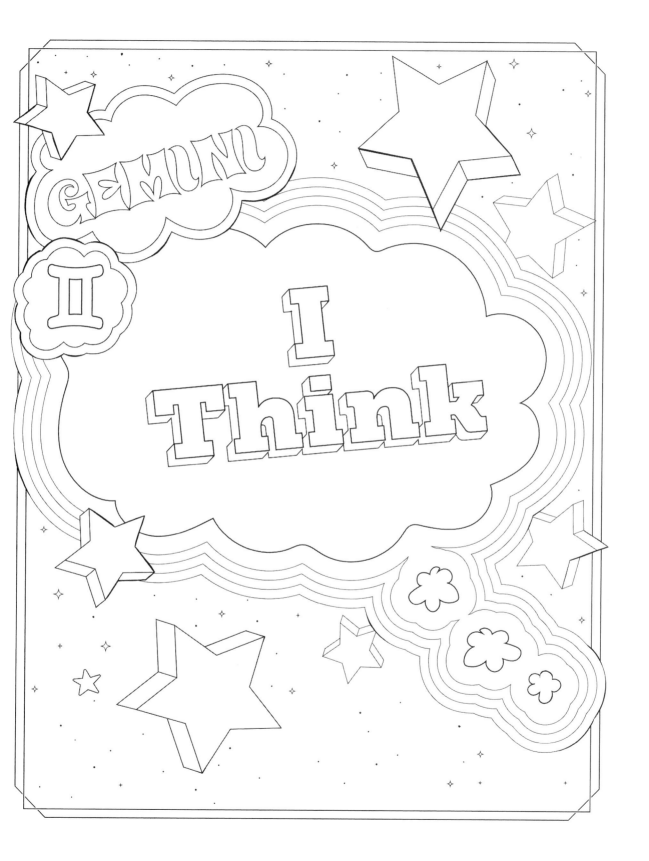

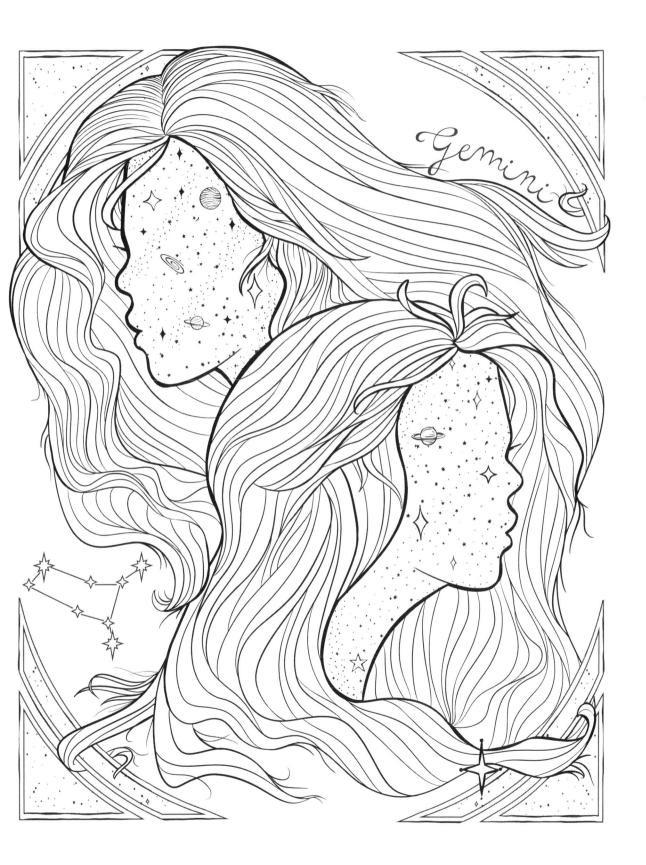

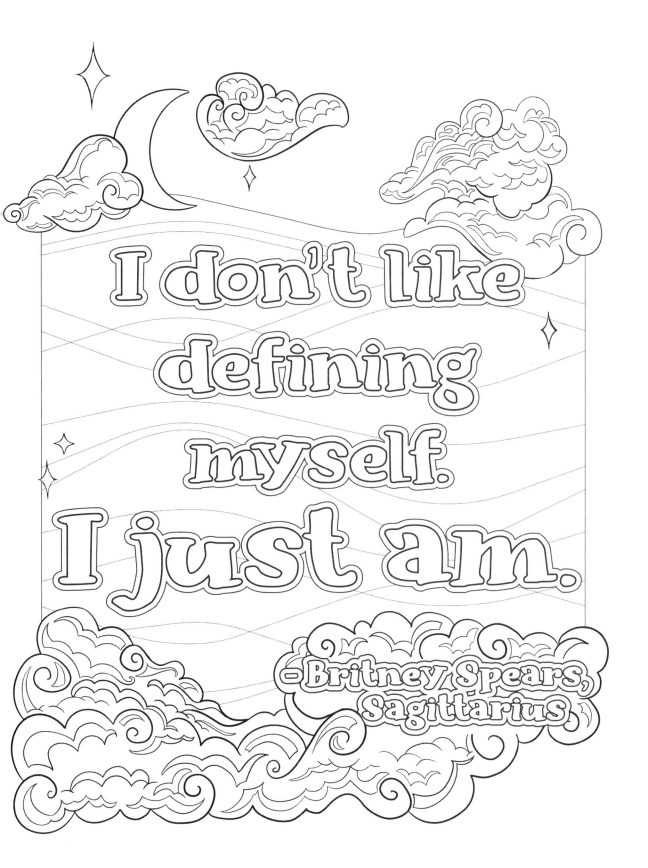

I don't like defining myself. I just am.

-Britney Spears, Sagittarius

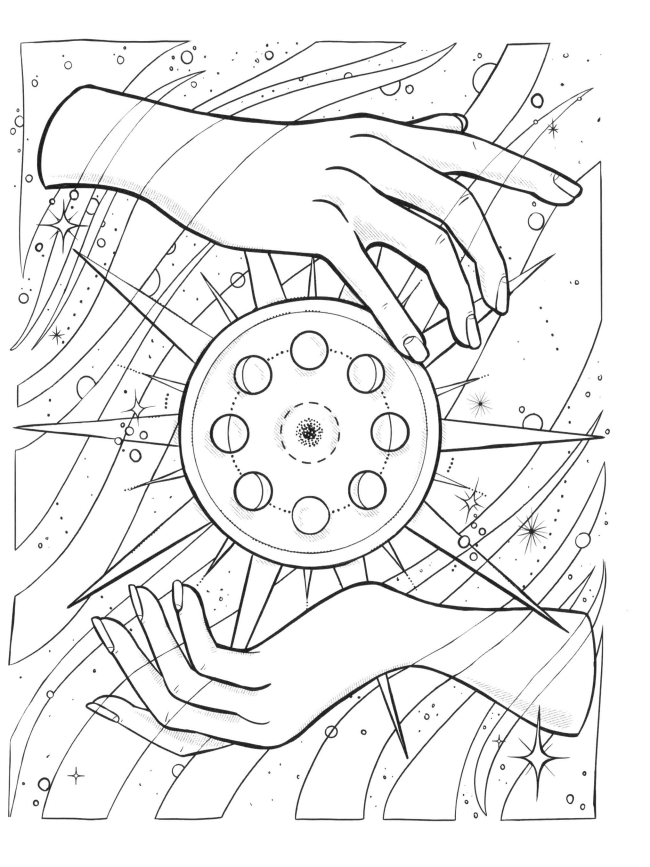

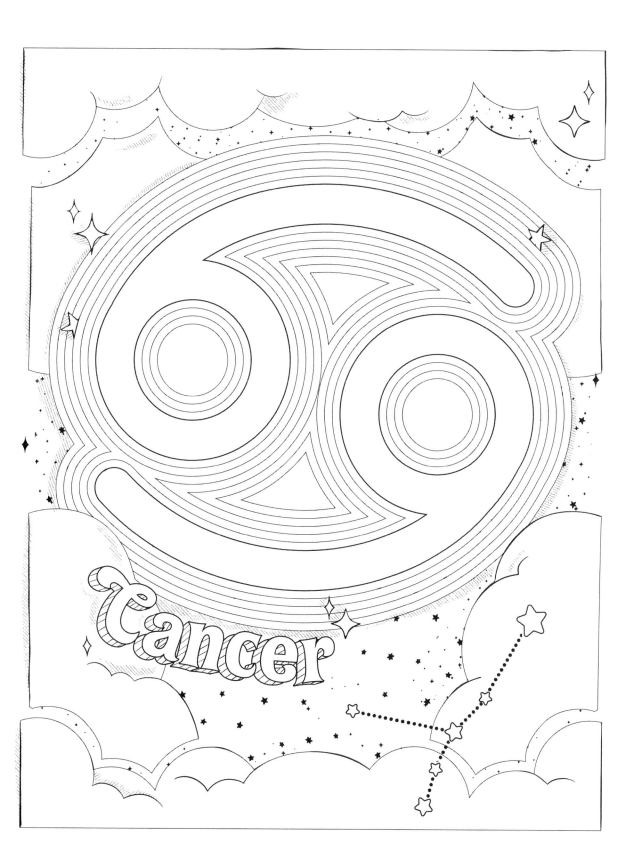

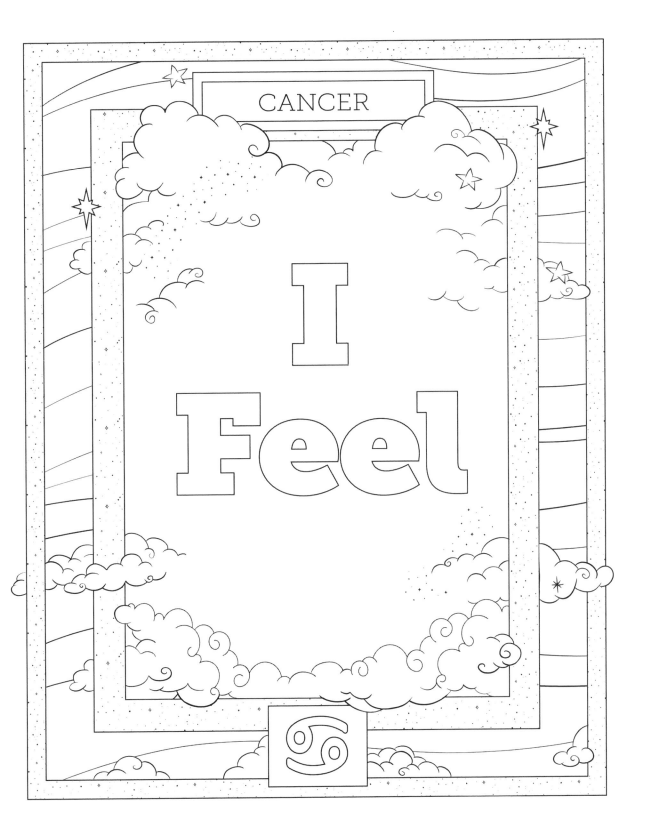

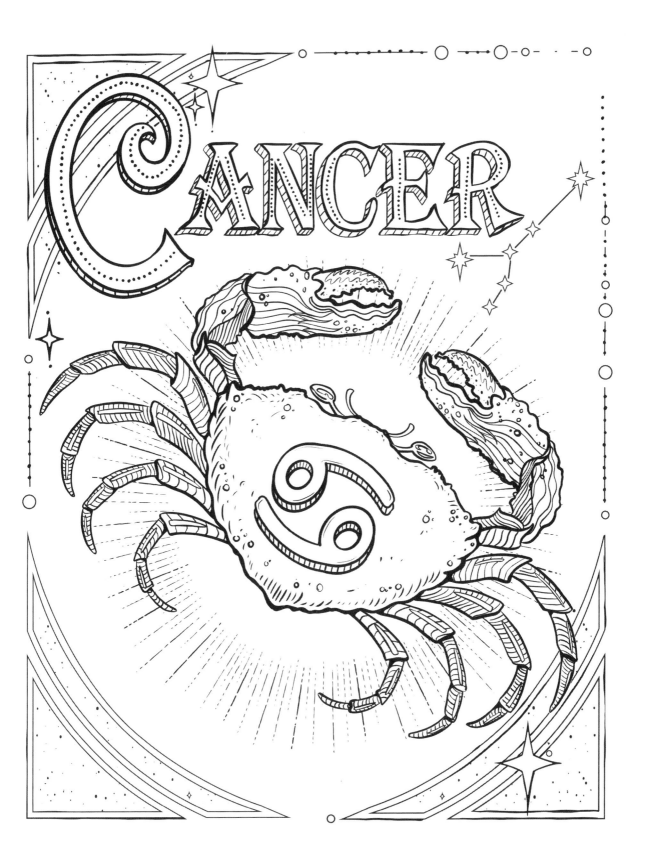

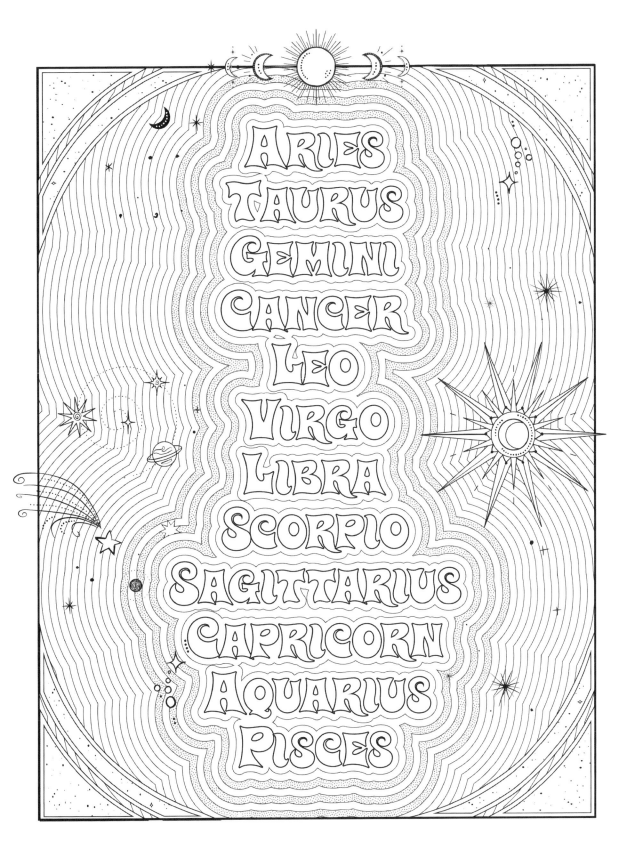

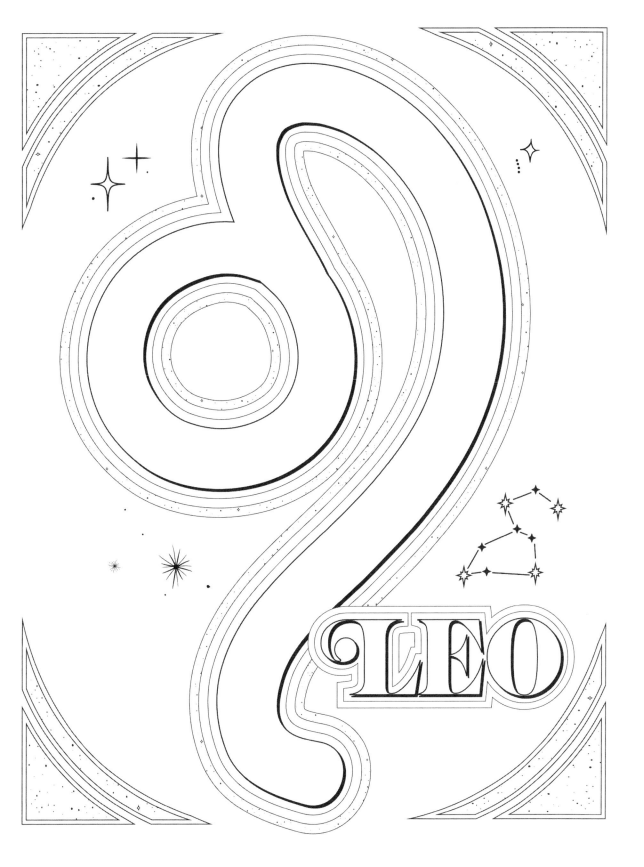

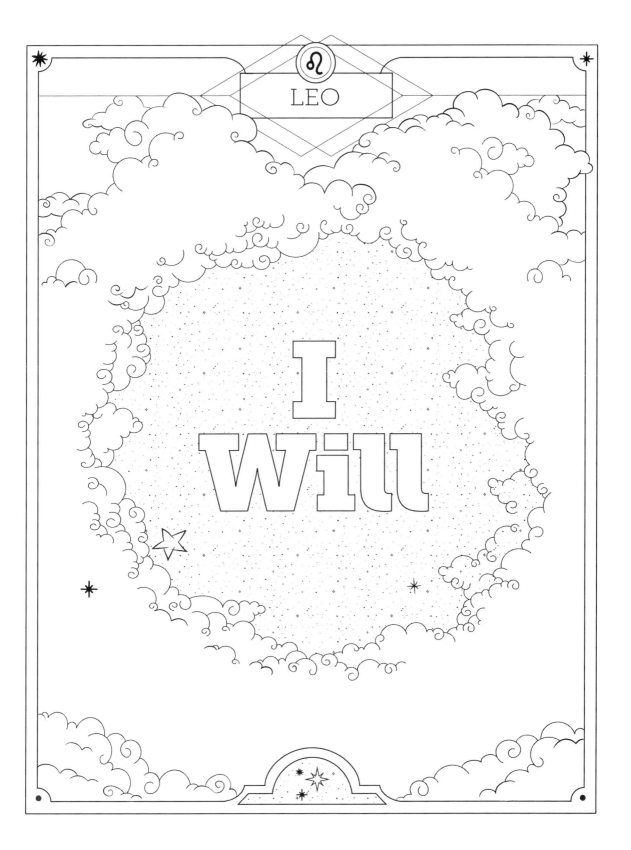

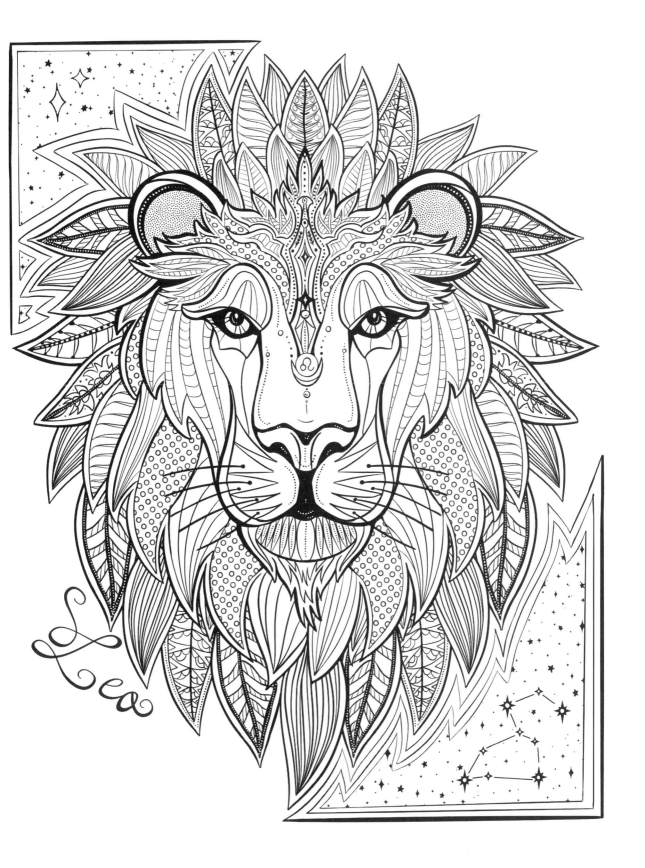

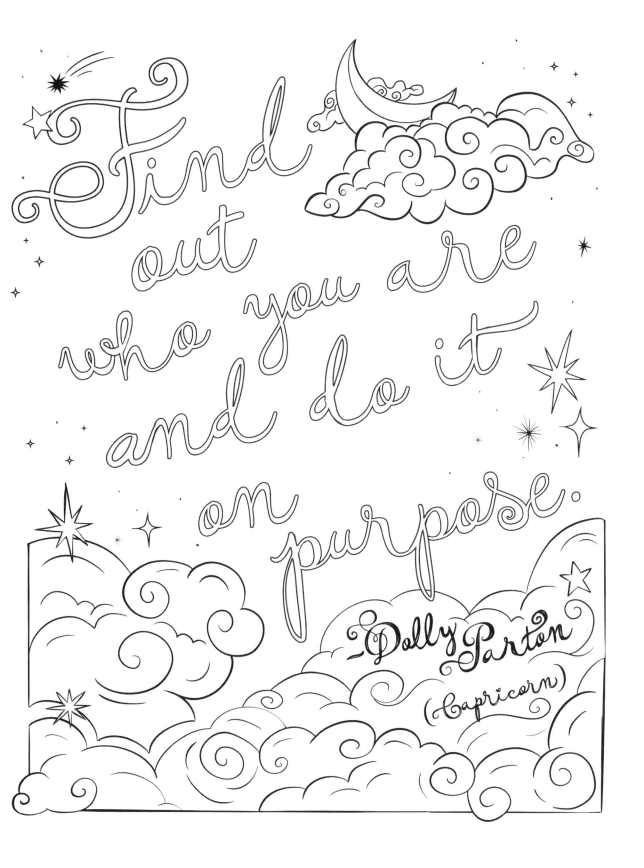

Find out who you are and do it on purpose.

—Dolly Parton (Capricorn)

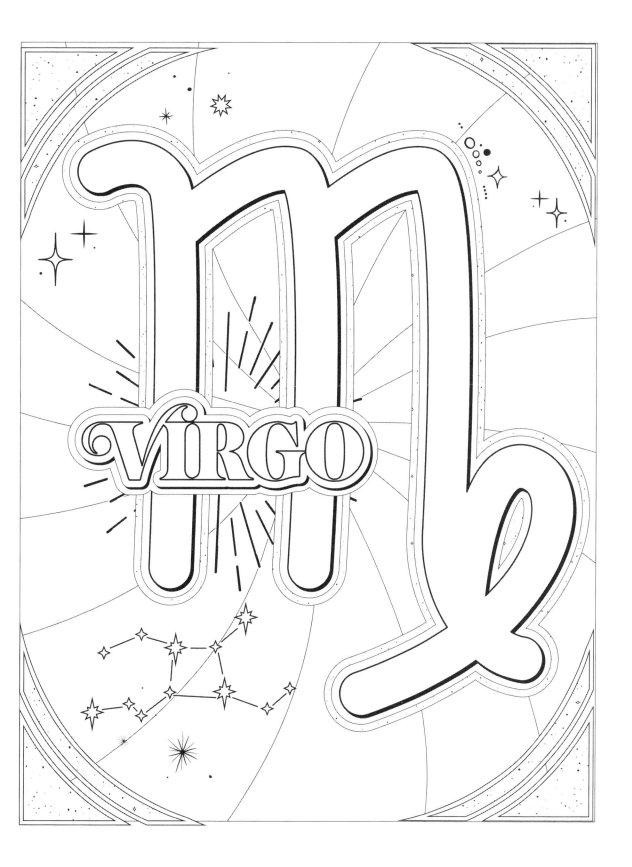

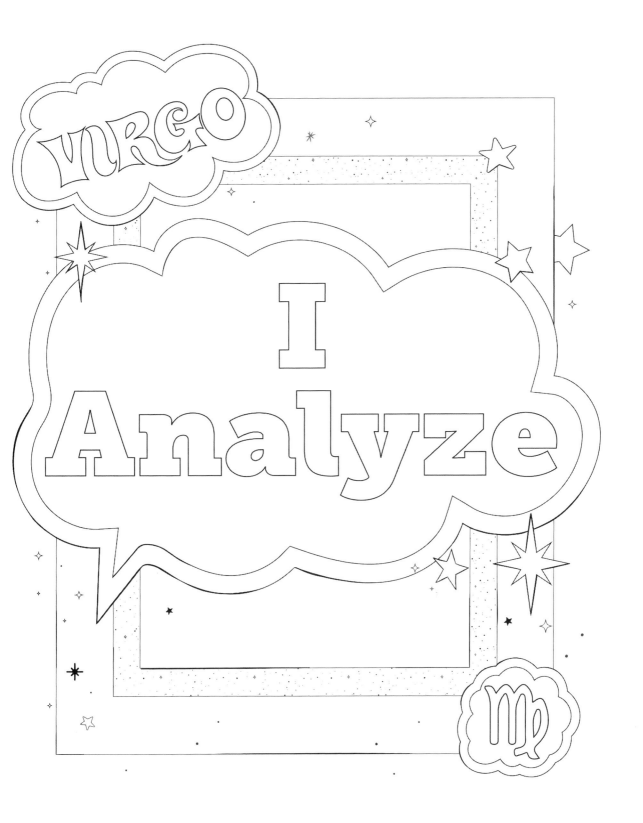

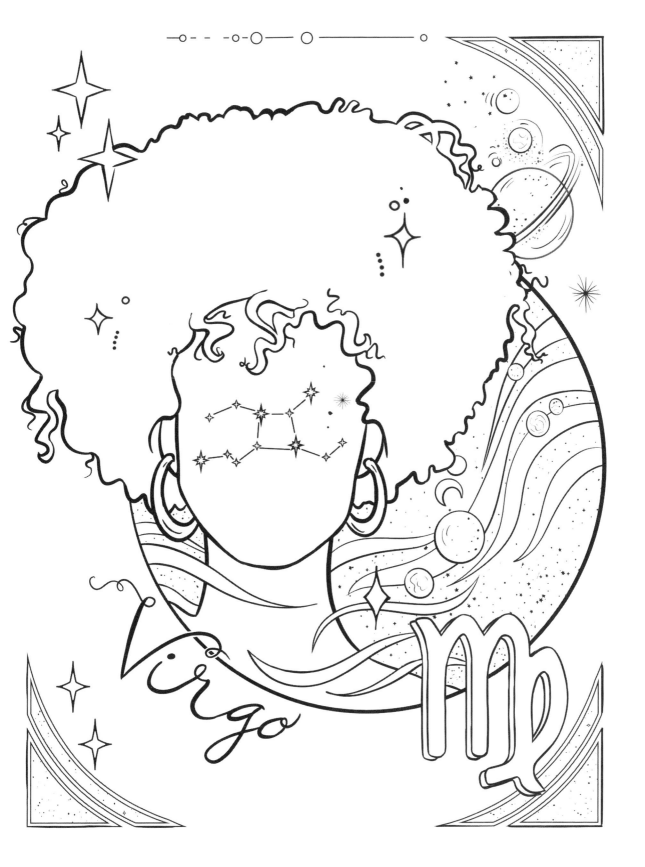

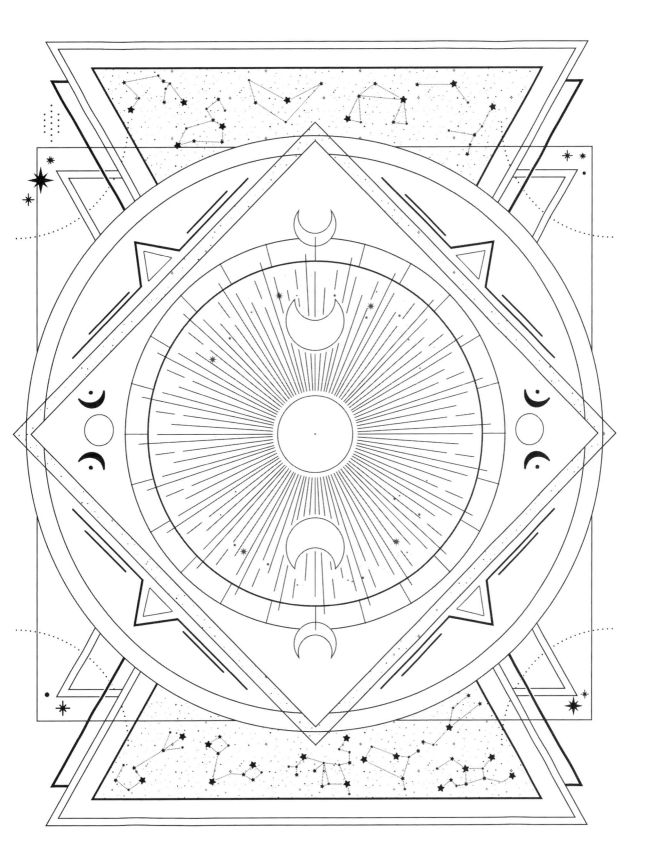

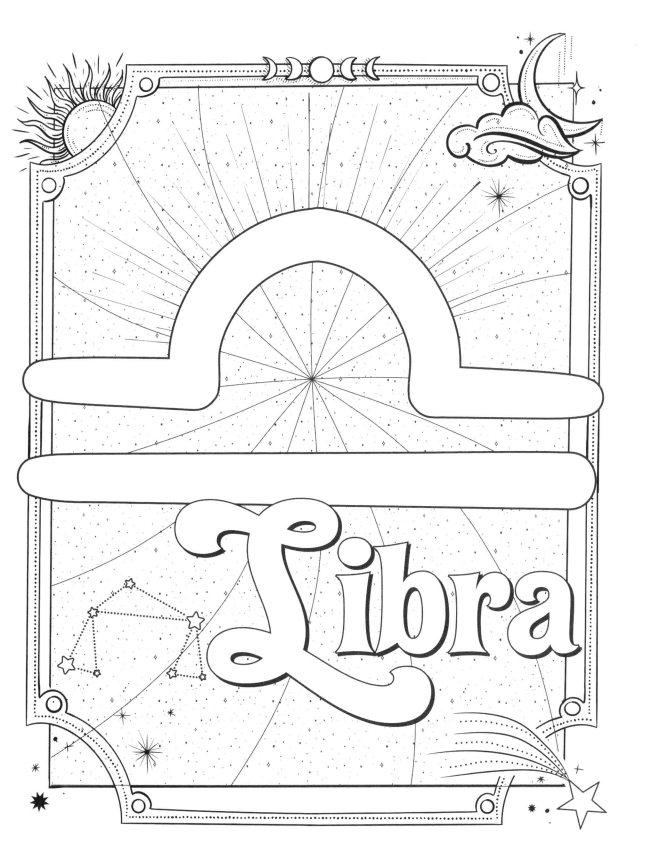

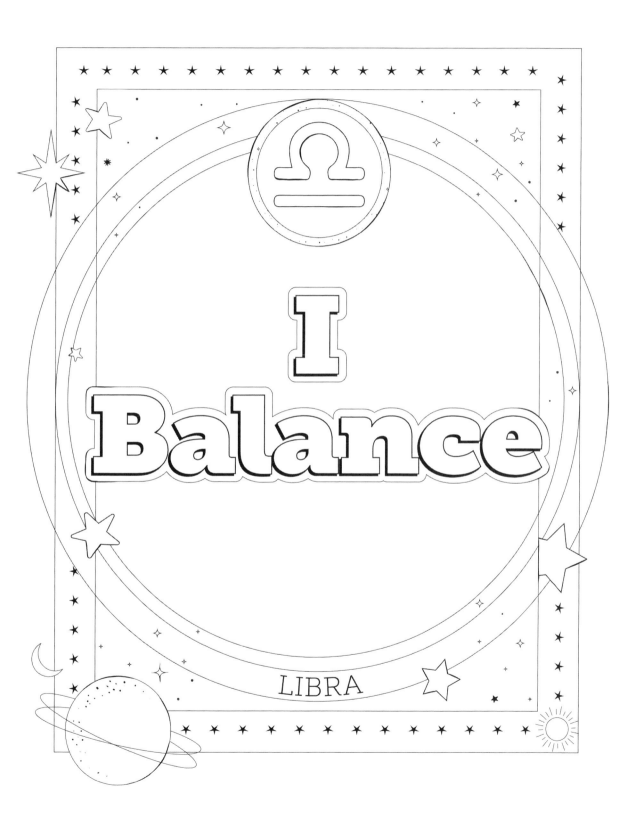

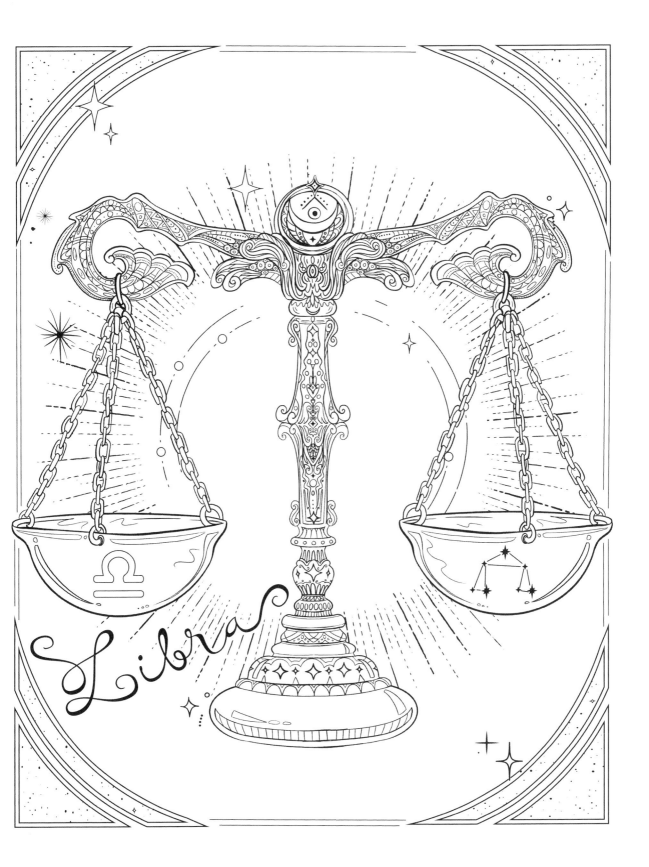

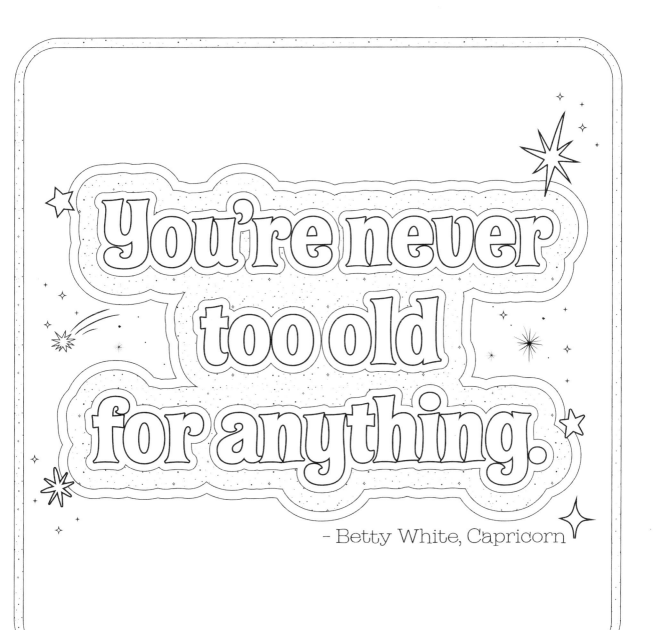

You're never too old for anything.

- Betty White, Capricorn

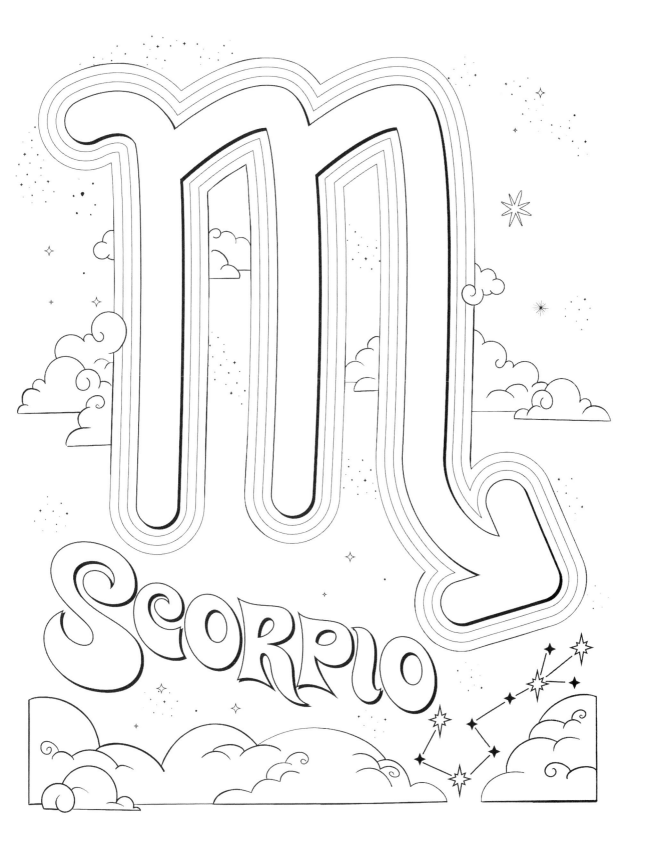

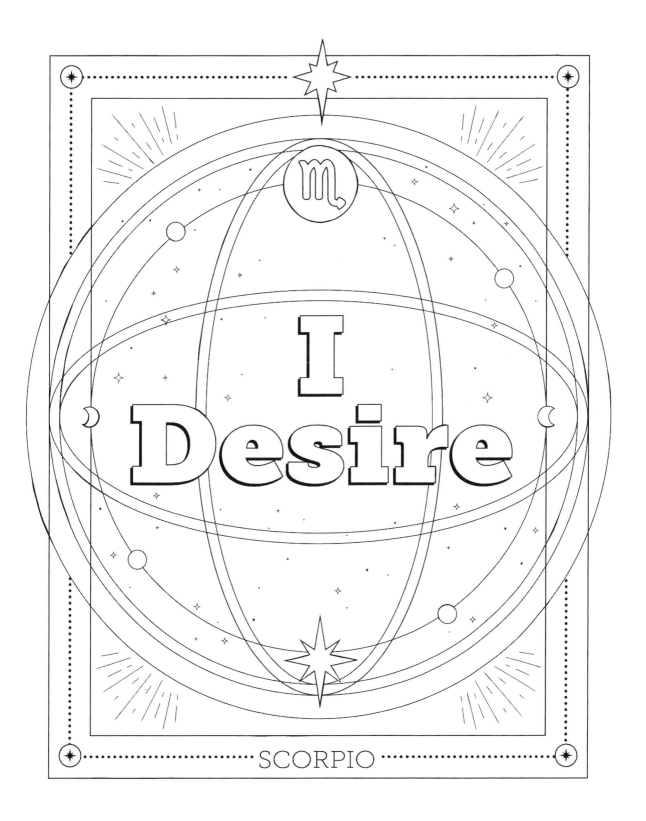

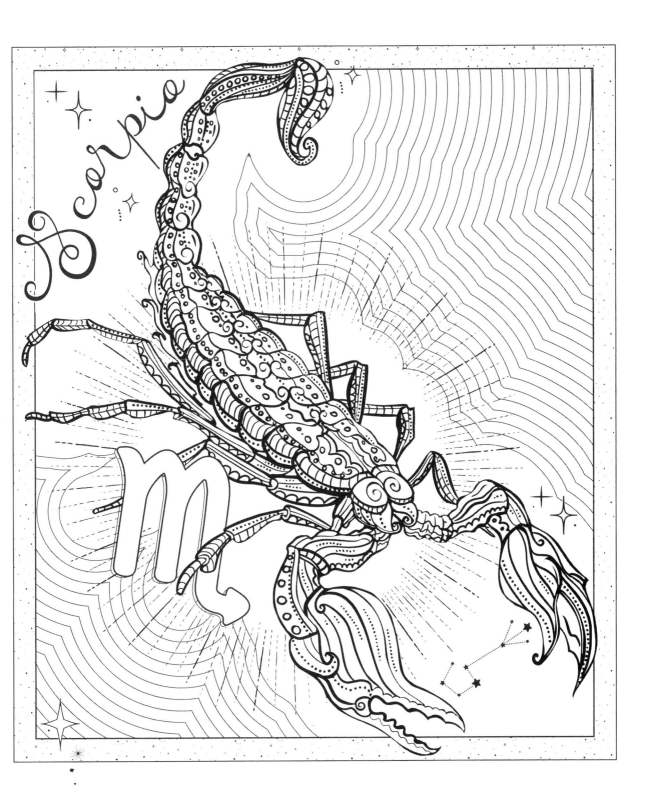

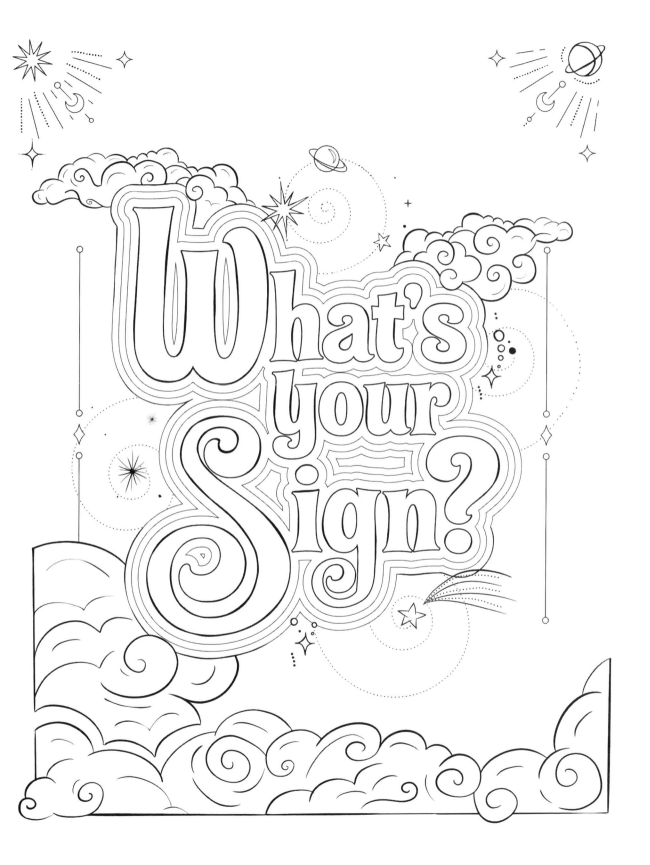

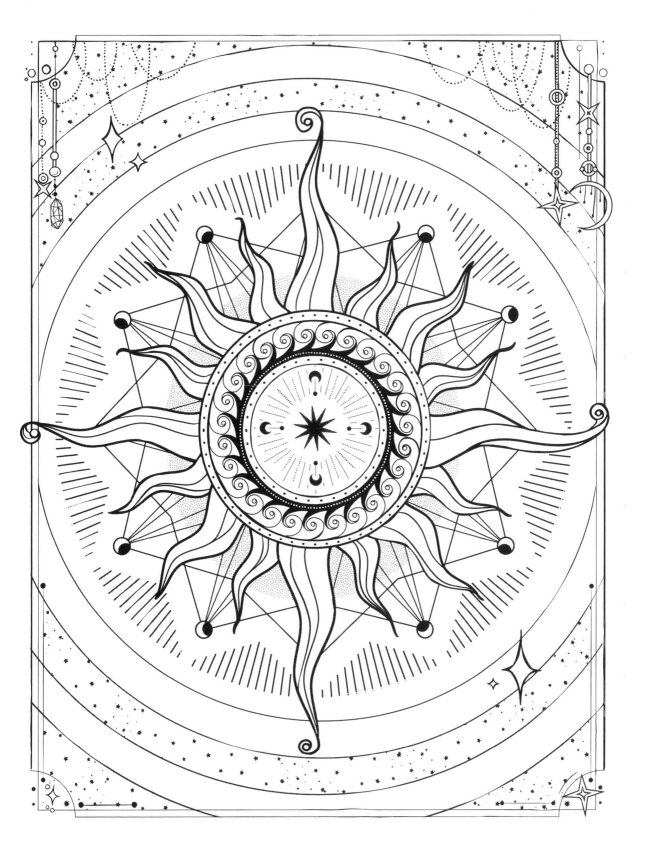

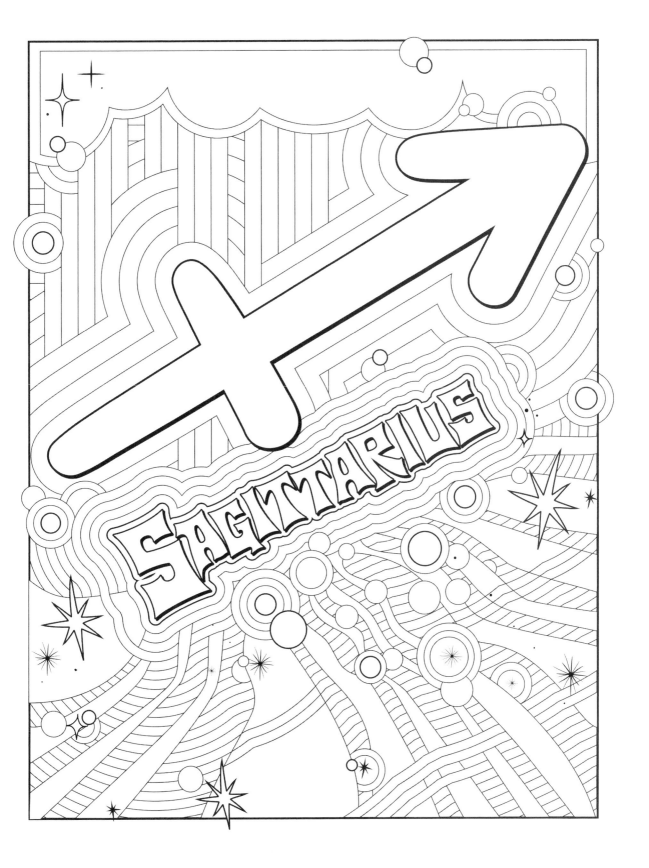

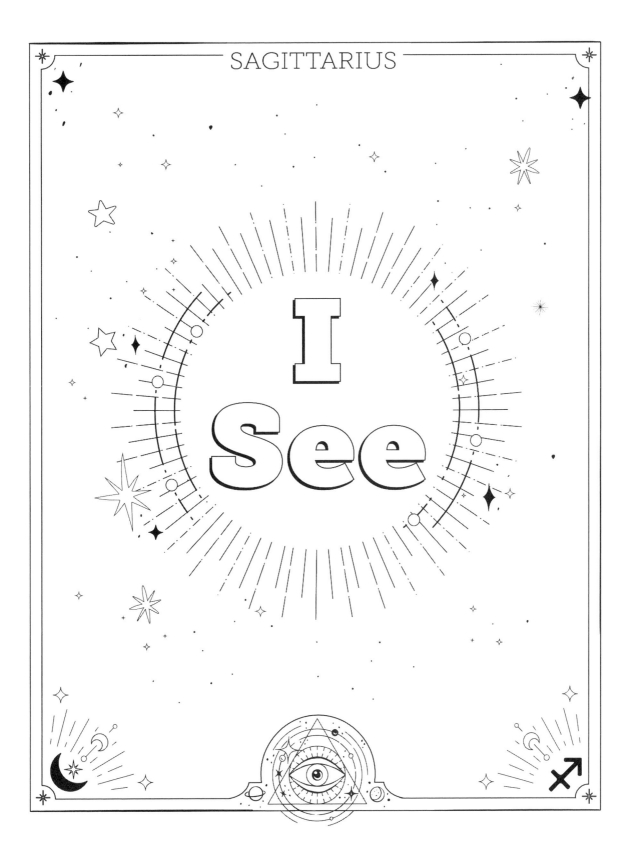

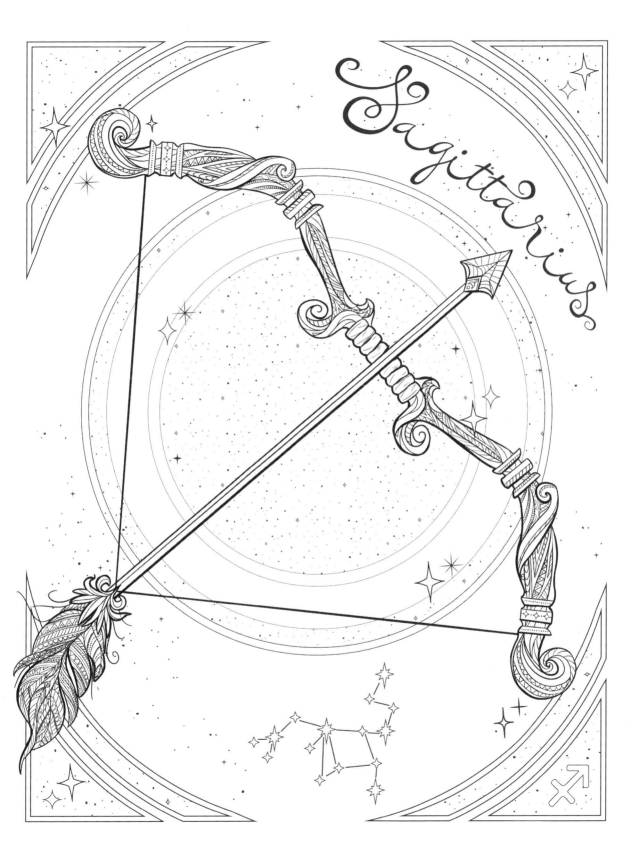

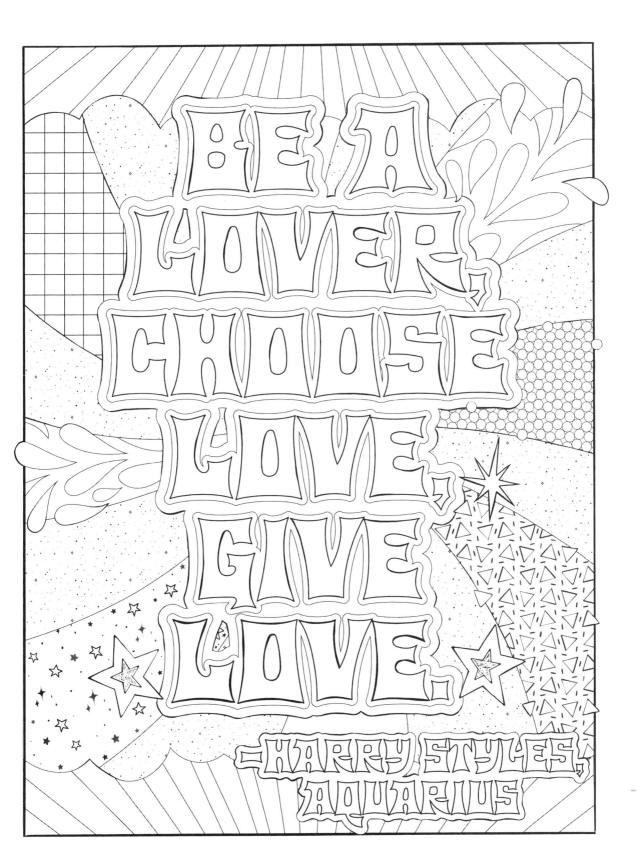

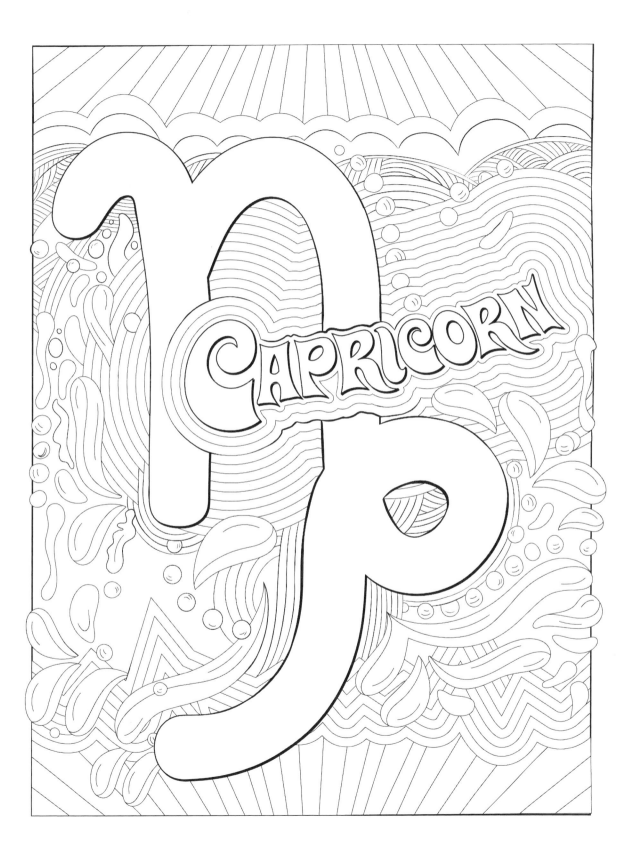

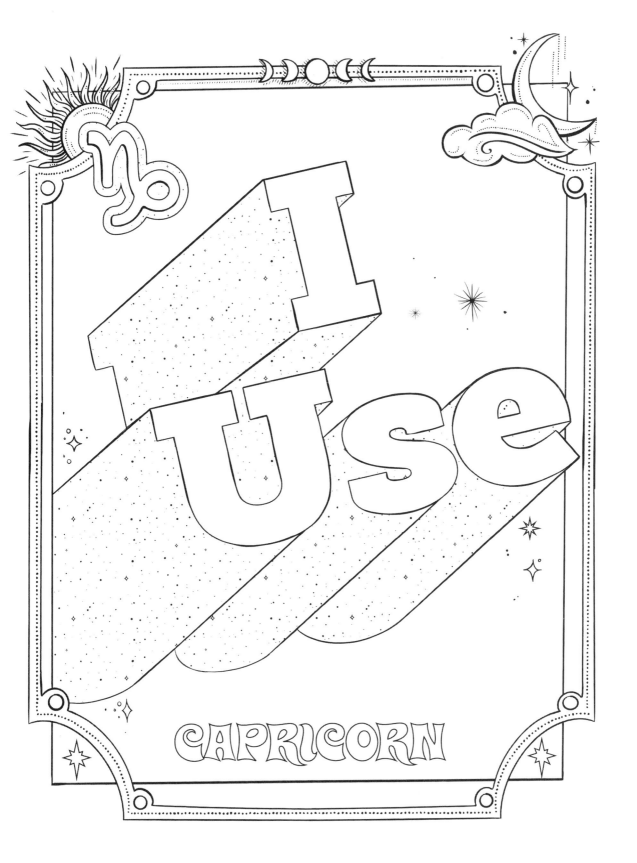

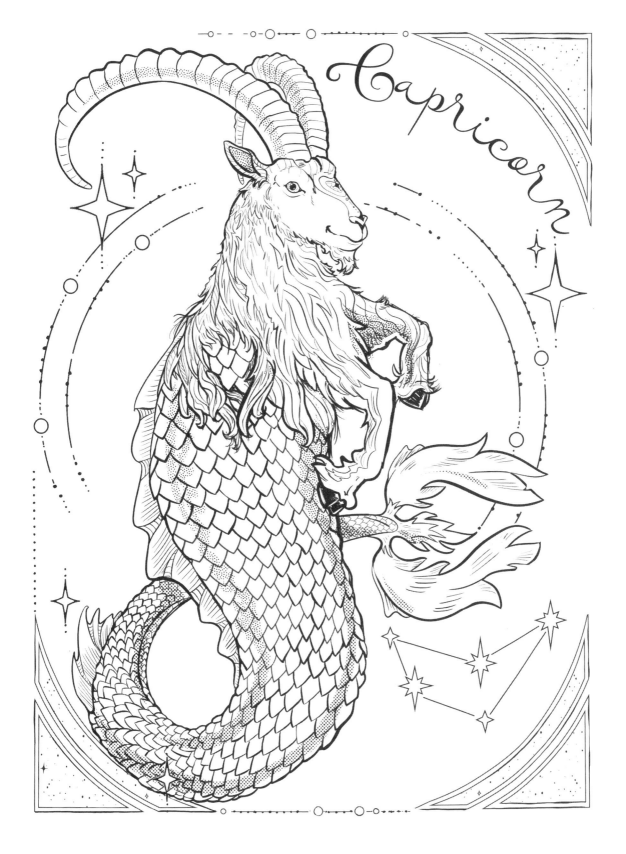

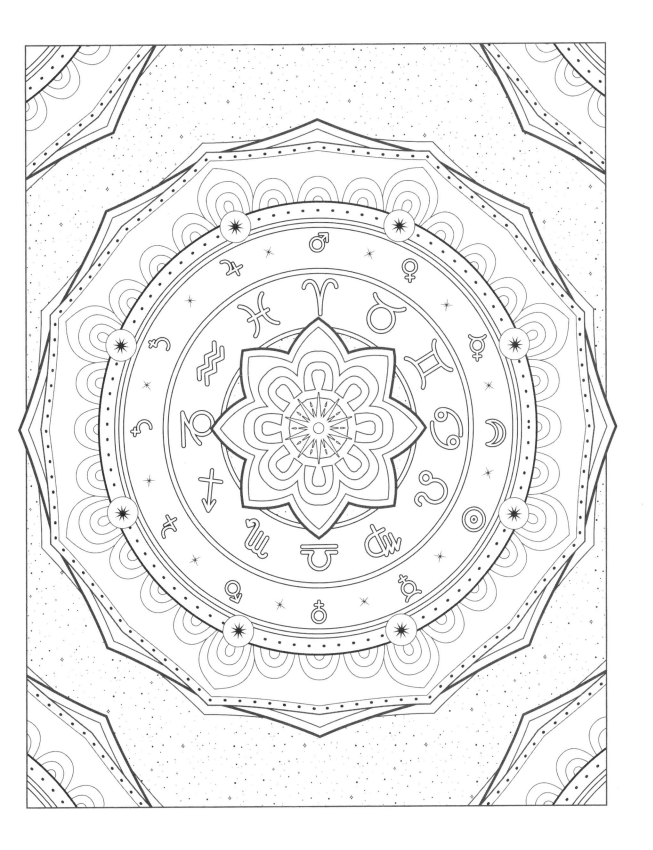

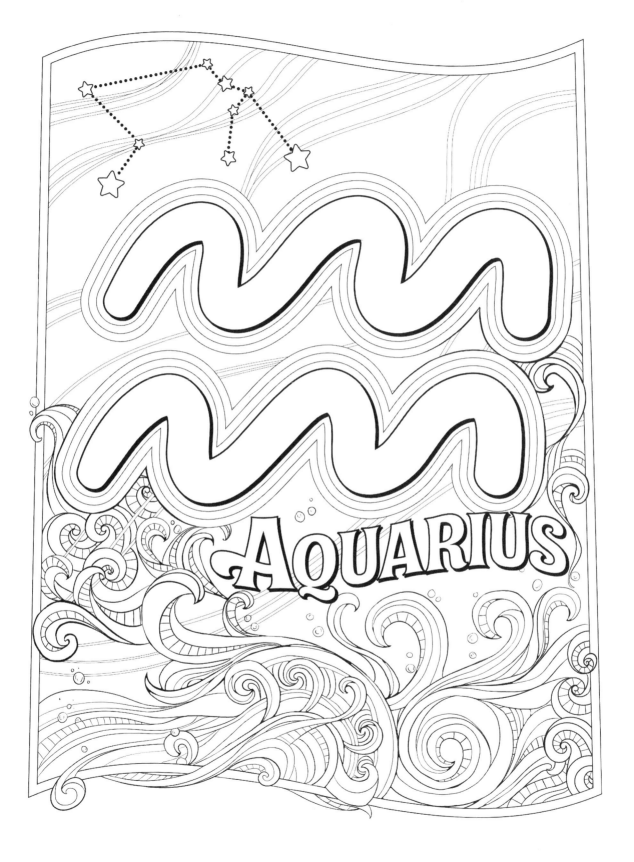

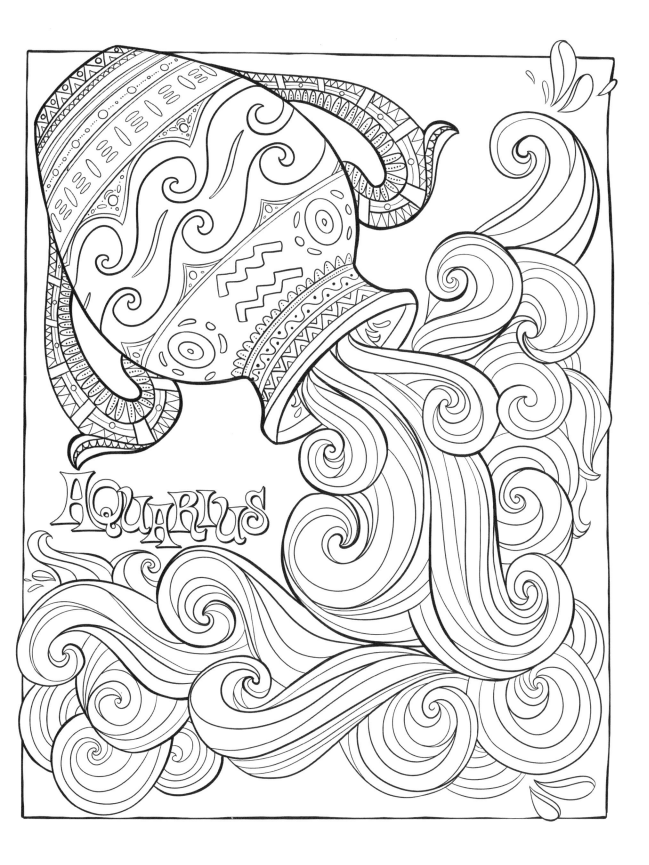

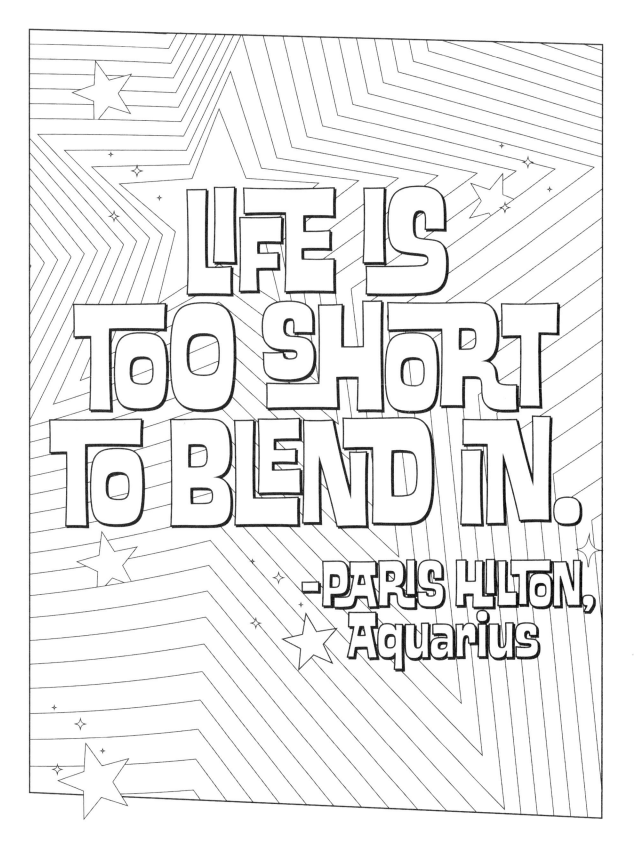

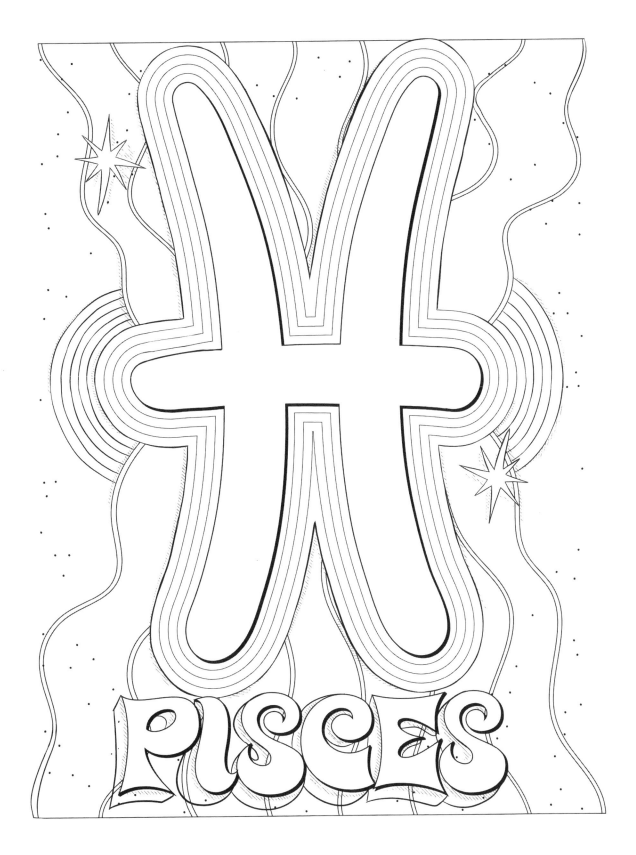

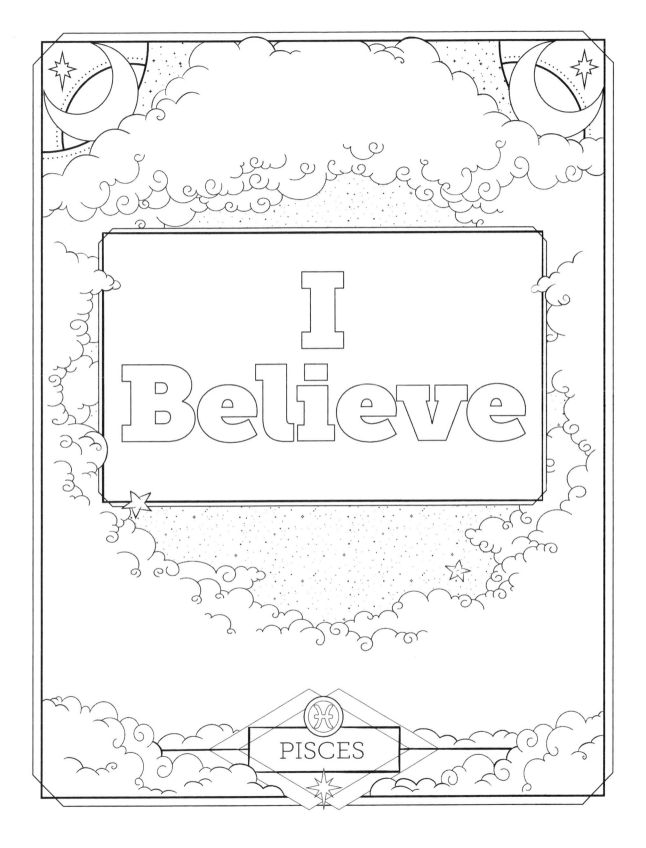

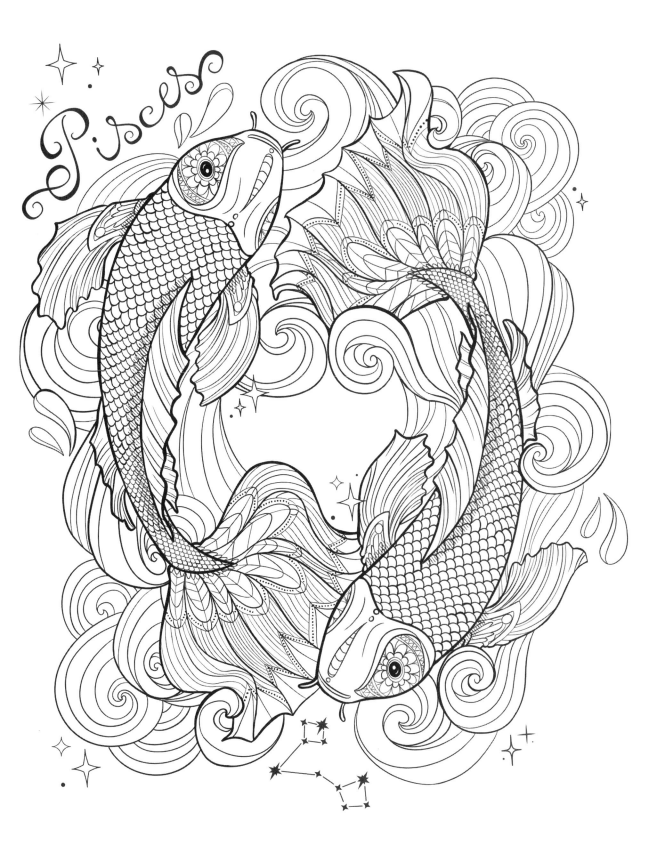

About the Author

Christina Haberkern is a designer and illustrator in Los Angeles. She is the owner and creative mind behind Hello Harlot, a stationery and gift-item brand specializing in pop culture and humorous products.